WICCA SYMBOLS FOR BEGINNERS

THE COMPLETE GUIDE TO SYMBOLOGY: Water, Fire, Colors, Essential Oils, Astrology, Self Care + Simple Spells

DAPHNE BROOKS

**Copyright - 2020
Daphne Brooks
All rights reserved.**

The content contained within this book may not be reproduced, duplicated or transmitted without direct written permission from the author or the publisher.

Under no circumstances will any blame or legal responsibility be held against the publisher, or author, for any damages, reparation, or monetary loss due to the information contained within this book. Either directly or indirectly.

Legal Notice:

This book is copyright protected. This book is only for personal use. You cannot amend, distribute, sell, use, quote or paraphrase any part, or the content within this book, without the consent of the author or publisher.

Disclaimer Notice:

Please note the information contained within this document is for educational and entertainment purposes only. All effort has been executed to present accurate, up to date, and reliable, complete information. No warranties of any kind are declared or implied. Readers acknowledge that the author is not engaging in the rendering of legal, financial, medical or professional advice. The content within this book has been derived from various sources. Please consult a licensed professional before attempting any techniques outlined in this book.

By reading this document, the reader agrees that under no circumstances is the author responsible for any losses, direct or indirect, which are incurred as a result of the use of information contained within this document, including, but not limited to, - errors, omissions, or inaccuracies.

TABLE OF CONTENTS

INTRODUCTION — 5

CHAPTER - 1
   What is Wicca — 13

CHAPTER - 2
   Difference between the wiccan
   religion and performing magic — 17

CHAPTER - 3
   Symbology — 23

CHAPTER - 4
   Simple spells you can cast — 47

CHAPTER - 5
   How to use the wicca to Self Help
   and Sefl Care — 51

CHAPTER - 6
   A bit of astrology — 63

CHAPTER - 7
   Wicca Altar and Tools
   and their symbology — 85

CONCLUSION — 93

INTRODUCTION

Over the years, the eyes of many have been opened to the most important truth of the century: we are all part of more substantial nature. And Wicca has a more significant role to play in it. Many things and events have tried to stifle this knowledge from the earth, but any real idea or religion has its way of returning to the surface.

There was a time when being a Wicca, which had a different name at that time, was an offense. But the present world has made it glaring that we can excel. Being a reviving culture or religion, a lot of people have made several suggestions through books, blogs, vlogs, and so many other media. These suggestions now make it hard for a new convert to enjoy the beauty of this religion.

In light of that, this book is aimed at guiding you through the different aspects of Wicca. As much as there is complex information everywhere. It had been simplified, and the knowledge is gleaned not only from personal experiences but from the knowledge and the skills of sages.

Written with you in mind, this book has been set to enlighten you, and that journey starts now.

A LITTLE BIT OF HISTORY

Wiccan is a religious practice that sprung up in the 1950s. the birth of Wicca began with Gardner and a few others who claimed to believe in the Wicca faith. According to this sect, they had been introduced into the faith by their ancestors. So, to them, their traditional religion was Wicca and as such, they struggled to keep the faith growing by doing what was expected of them.

Sybil Leek, Charles Cardell amongst others were the few that claimed that the Wicca faith was their traditional form of prayers. Coincidentally, their form of belief was similar to that practiced by Gardner. As such, it didn't take a long time for people to accept their views and explanations.

Many individuals settled to accept that the form of religion those individuals practiced were solely Wicca but for others, it was termed a traditional form of witchcraft. So, the practice was accepted to a minimal point.

WICCA TOOLS FOR BEGINNERS

The name "Wicca" was introduced by Charles Cardell. He didn't want to refer to the religion as some sort of witchcraft. So, he settled to refer to it as either Wicca or Wicen.

Thus the term "Wiccan" was used to refer to any witch-cult practice among the people. An attempt was made to reconcile all the witch – cult-based religions but the effort proved to be unrealistic and futile.
After a few years Gardner introduced Wiccan, it spread its tentacles across various populations and countries. The religion had suddenly spread across different countries like Scotland and Ireland. However, in the early part of the 1960s, the religion spread across the different English countries like the united states and Australia.

The religion thrived in Australia and the individuals welcomed with him with open arms because of their pagan attitude and worship ways unlike in the United States. In the United States, the Wicca religion was introduced by an English man and his wife.

The English man, Raymond Buckland, together with his wife, Rosemary who had just relocated to the USA had to accept the religion accepted the religion they were introduced into the faith in a ceremony in Britain. The couple went back to America and founded a coven where they were able to practice the Gardnerian religion by making use of the book of shadows. The coven was later managed by another couple and they referred to the book of shadows to initiate new members into the practice. This spurned to a lot of interest among the population of the United States and they decided to own their personal covens. This, in turn, helped to make the religion spread faster among the people of the United States as such it became easier to propagate the religion by the word of mouth rather than initiation.

Another form of religion was introduced in the United States in the 1960s and it was not in conformity with the Gardnerian practice. However, the first Wicca church became recognized in 1972. In 2000, the Wiccan practice also became popular with other countries like South Africa and India.

In the 1960s, a man emerged and claimed to be initiated into the witchcraft practice by his grandmother. The man was identified as Alex Sanders. After much research was carried out, it was proved that he had been initiated into the Gardnerian coven by his grandmother. The research also proved that his grandmother was experienced in crafting good crafts. His reputation also increased when he married Maxine Sanders.

The couple referred to themselves as the king and queen of witches. The couple had some witches and covens and also expanded their coven. At some point in time, Sanders combined both the elements of Wicca and Christianity together and this didn't go down well with the rest of the coven members. Sanders explained such a combination by stating that the fusion of both religions would help to combat the elements of satanic manipulations.

When some members insulted his motive and intention for fusing both religious practices, Sanders called it bluff and stated that they were not being knowledgeable in their actions. In the year 1973, the marriage between Alex and Maxine was annulled as a result of Alex's bisexuality.

Rather than a change from being a bisexual, Alex focused his attention on how to incorporate homosexual men into the religion. He sought to create ways the religion can accommodate homosexuals. At some point in time, he realized his follies ad apologized for his past mistakes. He also made attempts to create a fusion between Gardnerian and Sanders, but he later gave up the ghost in 1988.

The United States witnessed a lot of forms of Wiccan practices in 1970. The proponent of Wicca at this period tried to fuse the Gardnerian and Sanders practice of Wicca and this caused quite a stir among the believers who thought that it wasn't supposed to be so. Raymond Buckland who introduced the religion to the United States also left the practice and introduced another type of practice.

The seax- Wiccan was introduced by Raymond so that any willing person could practice. He also made available its rites and rituals and documented it in a book.

Budapest came up with a form of Wiccan practice that encouraged the females to practice religion with fear or favor. This form of Wiccan was largely referred to as a feminist approach to Wiccan.

This approach was made to embrace females into practicing the religion irrespective of their lineage. So, any willing female was at the right of practicing the religion without any restriction whatsoever. The Dianic approach to Seax was more to honor a goddess.

Wiccans are always expected to swear an oath of secrecy that would restrict them from discussing the activities of their rituals to anybody. The Gardnerian practice of Wiccan did not comply with this oath. Rather, they preferred to carry out their rituals in the full glare of the people without pretense.

This went on for a while until there was some sort of misconception about the Wiccan practice. A lot of people started to attribute the practice to a lot of evil and darkness. So, to prevent these situations, the Wiccans decided to reveal its operations to the general public and avoid the unpleasant situation of attributing the practice to something evil.

Suddenly, Wiccan became more pronounced than it ever was. A lot of people got to know about the Wiccan religion and sought to become members of the cult. The entertainment was not left out as it made some movies that revolved around Wiccan religion and practices. One of the movies produced by the entertainment sector didn't reveal the real intent of the Wiccan religion and depicted a bad image of the religion. So, to curb these effects and unwanted imagery of the practice, the various Wiccan covens placed a strict restriction on the acceptance of members into their coven.

The age limit for participation became eighteen years and above. This made it difficult for inquisitive teenagers to gain entry into the coven. As such, they turned to their books to seek answers to the questions that plagued their hearts. Of course, the books provided all the needed information to satisfy the curiosity of various individuals.

A lot of teenagers are interested in religion because it addresses issues that a lot of other religions do not address adequately. This has caused an uproar among different practitioners who feel that teenagers are not expected to participate in the practice. To worsen the situation, a certain twelve –year- old teen was killed as a result of practicing the faith.

The presence of the internet also worsened the situation and made Wicca get a large ground of popularity. As a matter of fact, Wiccan was regarded as a common witch- cult and didn't get enough recognition but today in virtually every major city, Wicca is greatly permissible. The Wiccan is not just any other cult, but it is now regarded as a religion. It has successfully integrated different parts and sects of people together. The interest of a lot of practitioners has successfully caused the religion to gain recognition. As a matter of fact, there was a case of a Wiccan wedding in the year 2004. The Wiccan wedding was performed in the United Kingdom.

WICCA TOOLS FOR BEGINNERS

CHAPTER - I

WHAT IS WICCA?

Wicca is culture modelled after the traditions in existence before the coming of Christianity into Ireland, Scotland, and Wales.

You can call it having a deep connection to the nature around us. It is appreciating things like the sunrise, sunset, or the little things around us. You might find joy in such thing as the way the morning dew is balanced on the petals of a flower.

In essence, Wicca is when one finds joys in the healing of others through natural means, seeking or protecting the natural things. It might even be when you have the desire to teach others about the intricacy of the naturalness of life.

ORIGIN OF WICCA

To take a more in-depth look at Wicca is to firstly understand that the processes defined up there had been at the pre--Christianity era. They have been used in the healing of people and had been used to improved several medical knowledge. However, unlike Christianity, many of these great understandings were not thoroughly documents.

Thus, when Christianity entered these high countries of the United Kingdom, it was easy to blot out some information. In reality, the word Wicca actually was the initial way of referring to witches at those times.

However, when nomenclature moved from town to town, there was a shift in the pronunciation, making the name change from what it had been known for.

In fact, through the help of archaeologists, it is believed that this belief system emanated from the worship of Hunter god and a fertility goddess by the Palaeolithic people. These archaeologists traced their existence to about 30,000 years ago.

Their discovery was made through the study of such things as cave paintings. The painting depicted a man who had a head of a stag and a pregnant woman in a circle created by eleven people.

It is no longer news that a lot of information had been

lost in the Christianity era, but many people have made several deductions and cold calculation that has helped in restricting the system. Thus, it can be concluded that Wicca is focused on the beliefs in the worship of the god and goddess. Anyone with the knowledge of Wicca is prone to study more about herbs and have a wide range of education in lines of medicine. In the days of predating Christianity, many witches were among the Shaman.

In ancient history, there was a sort of respect accorded Wiccans because witchcraft was regarded as a craft of the wise. One primary reason was that they were tuned to nature and had a vast knowledge of herbs and medicine, making them a very essential part of the survival of the villages or communities they reside in.

Because of their understanding of how human was just a part of the whole elements of nature, they have a way of reminding people of this salient point: humans were not superior to other aspects of life but are simply a part of the whole process. Thus, they always tend to help in the creation of balance and equilibrium of life. There is every assurance that the modern man has lost this value and have placed a higher value on the superiority of the existence of humans.

And we can clearly see this in the recent happenings around us including the ecological disasters around us as well the extinction of individual animals because of the human greed and desire for material wealth.

This problem has its consequence; the eventual destruction of some unique animals or insects might lead to the extinction of the human species.

The past hundred years have unfortunately painted a bad image of witches. For some reason, they have been regarded as evil, unrighteous, and heathen. These misconceptions, however, emanated from centuries into the coming of Christianity.

When the medieval church began in the 15 century, certain myths were propagated among people, especially followers of this religion. The underlying message was that their faith was filled with evil and oppressive methods.

Their mind was warped to believe they have been using diabolical means into the creation of balance. In other words, their servitude and reverence of nature were regarded as service to devils and demons.

The missionary projected fear on the mind of people and made them suspicious of their gods because many of them were regarded as demon-filled deities. In fact, tales and imaginations were built around witches as wicked people.

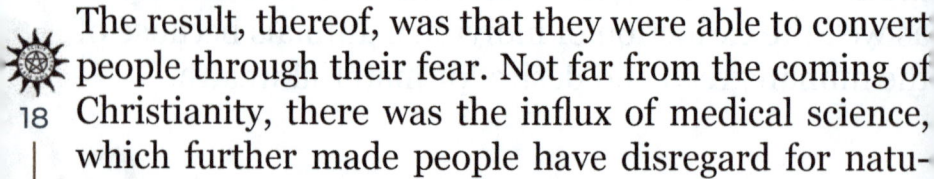

The result, thereof, was that they were able to convert people through their fear. Not far from the coming of Christianity, there was the influx of medical science, which further made people have disregard for nature-based worship. Medical science, however, allowed people to have a standardized study of the human body, thus disregarding the potency of nature-based worship. The studies that had been carried out on several occasions were done by men, who were oblivious to many of the many problems faced by women.

This ignorance was one of the tools used by the church. Several of the missionaries were really vast in the knowledge of science and could easily fault the knowledge of the witches. The credence they got made it easy for the church to seem superior and this proved their erroneous beliefs as right, giving their witch hunt credibility.

The misinformation further went on to hold a lot of people bound that it was easy to stop some traditions that many are yearning for its existence today. Looking at the glimpse of some of these traditions has proved itself to something the world needs today, but the knowledge is just limited. Now, to further understand these traditions by juxtaposing events with one another, Wicca started.

The adoption of the name, however, came in to avoid the numerous persecution that came with the name with. This psychology even went as far as those that weren't Christians at that time.

This hideous image of witches remained in the series of events that have been enunciated movies and books.

Many of the entertainment had tried to depict witches evil. To a large extent, this superstition had crossed several centuries and have found a resting place in the heart of several people on a day like.

To avoid the numerous persecution, harassment, as well as the misinformation linked to the name witch, the group decide to remain known as Wicca.

WICCA TOOLS FOR BEGINNERS

CHAPTER - 2
Difference between the wiccan religion and performing magic

Performing Magic can be trying to create an illusion of bringing out effects. Doing or performing magic can actually be a trick to make one believe that there is a vast improvement or change in the ways things are done. However, upon a closer look, you can discover that there is a difference in the ways things are done and that can effectively be the cause of some misconceptions about power.

Wiccan religion, on the other hand, is being tuned to nature and seeing oneself a means of balancing the world. That way, anything done is used with the realism of nature in mind. The creation of things can only happen at the heart of nature.

One other major difference between Wiccan and doing magic is that one the former is a religion. For any religion to function correctly, it must be a set of people operating under the same types of beliefs. Thus, we can say that while doing or performing magic is a practice, Wiccan is a religion.

Remember that when referring to religion, you are talking about some sets of methodologies used in getting results. In Wiccan, further studies are done to question and answer life's reality. But Magic is mainly done for entertainment or creation of things that have not been in a long while. As a Wiccan, one is made to observe certain rites to a deity or spirit or even worship them. As a Wiccan, you can also make specific prayers, meditation, healing, or even perform magic.

However, anyone performing magic is not tied to a particular religion. Modern magic is gotten from books or blogs and can be practiced without the need to make obeisance to any god or spirit. We can conclude that it is had nothing attached like the other one. You might not even need the power of a witch to perform certain magic as long as you can follow the methods to the letter.

Magic is the end game of anyone performing it but for the Wiccans, practicing magic is one of the requirements needed for the process of worshiping their gods. In fact, there have been arguments pointing to the fact that prayer is magic. Looking at it from the overall level, we can factually say that the major difference between the two is the intent.

The primary intention of Magic is to perform things for entertainment while the other one is to become attuned to nature and everything that is involved. Wiccan focus on worship, the lord, and the lady. They also make an observation of the turn of the Wheel of the year. They not only do that, but they also pay much attention to the spirituality of the person performing magic.

Magic is detached and has no emotional attachment to their performance. Many of them are even done to trick others as the basic concept is to understand the methods and the right things to say or do when performing any trick.

CHAPTER - 3
Symbology

We will explore the symbols of significant aspects you will always encounter as a Wiccan.
They are
- Symbolism of Elements

DIFFERENT THINGS MAKE UP ELEMENTS, BUT OUR FOCUSES ARE ON WATER, FIRE, AND AIR

- o Water
- o Fire
- o Air
- Symbolism of Color
- Symbolism of Essential Oil

SYMBOLISM OF WATER

The symbolism of water is so many that they can only be summarized here. Like the water in the world, you cannot fully comprehend the deepest meaning of water symbols. Compared to the deep sea, its purpose has several layers of deepness.

When using them for different things like dreams, intuition, magic, or mystery, you will find eternal inspiration from water. If you think about it, much of the deepest waters are still unexplored, which makes the meaning of water full of potential.

Keywords used several to symbolize water:

- Life
- Motion
- Renewal
- Blessing
- Intuition
- Reflection
- Subconscious
- Fertilization
- Purification
- Transformation

Water In Life

The symbolism of water has a universal undertone of purity and fertility. It is seen as one major source of life because of the numerous story that has trended around it being the place through which several creative processes began.

Among the first peoples of North America, water was regarded as a valuable commodity, especially in the more arid plains and western regions. Thus, the Native Americans accept it as a symbol of life, further solidifying the symbol affixed in many creation myths.

So, it is also with the ancient Egyptians as we learn their beloved (and heavily relied upon) Nile river is akin to the birth canal of their existence.

It is also interesting to note that the human body has more water than even blood. So, we can liken many of these myths and allegories to our own existence. Not that alone, when looking at water from the aspect of life, we will discover its symbolism of circulation, life, cohesion, and birth by associating the creative waters of the earth with the fluids found in our own body (i.e., blood).

Wisdom In Water

Taoist tradition believes that water is an aspect of wisdom. The theory here is that water does not have a shape just like wisdom. It can easily be formed through anything, and the same can be said of wisdom, which can even be gotten from a child. Like wisdom, water moves in the path of least resistance. Here the symbolic meaning of water speaks of a higher wisdom we may all aspire to mimic.

The ever-observant ancient Greeks understood the power of transition water holds. From liquid to solid, to vapor – water is the epitomic symbol for metamorphosis and philosophical recycling.

Water Symbolism in Astrology

Astrologically, we can find the symbolism of water through the zodiac signs.

- Cardinal water sign of Cancer (the crab) indicates purity, clarity, and refreshment
- Fixed water sign of Scorpio (the scorpion) speaks of mystery, stillness, and reflection.
- Mutable water sign of Pisces (the fish) indicates depth, motion, and life

Water Symbolism in Tarot

In the Tarot, we find water is symbolized by the entire suit of cups. Here, water is symbolic of emotion, intuition, and the interconnected flow of energy between all things alive. Some of the other cups are the moon (subconscious), star (intuition), and temperance (harmony with cycles).

Water Symbolism in the Celtic Ogham

Within the symbolic language of trees, we see the symbolism of cycles, revitalization, generosity as well as dreaming and visions.

In the Celtic realm of the Ogham, the following trees are associated with water: reed, alder, willow.

ELEMENTAL CORRESPONDENCES OF FIRE

Fire is active, warm, dry, bright, and masculine. It can be represented on the altar with a candle or a fire bowl or a blade.

Head: Corresponding Name

Season: Summer

Day: Sunday

Moon: Phase Waxing

Time: Noon

Archangel: Micheal

Chakra: Solar Plexus

Incense: Cinnamon, Frankincense, dragon's blood

Sabbats: Beltane, Samhain, Midsummer , Lughnassadhe

Zodiac: Signs Aries, Leo, Sagittarius

Animals: Lion, dragon, salamander, snakes, coyote, fox, mantids, scorpion, phoenix, ram, squirrel

Symbolic Posture: Standing straight forming a triangle over the head with arms

Major Arcana Tarot: Card Judgment (XX)

Minor Arcana: Suit Wands

Planets: Mars, Sun, Pluto

Elemental Spirits: Salamanders, Sprites, Djinn

Part of the Body: Head

Colors: White, Red, Orange, Gold, Scarlet, Crimson, Fuchsia, Maroon

Symbols: Flame, Sun, Star s, Volcanoes, Lightning bolt, Double-headed Axe (Labrys)

Goddesses: Brigit, Freya, Hestia, Pele, Vesta, Durga, Elena, Aetna, Yansa, Themis

Gods: Vulcan, Ra, Agni, Hephaestus, Horus, Atar, Chu-Jung, Mars, Aten

WICCA TOOLS FOR BEGINNERS

Magickal Tool: Fire, Wand, Lamp, athame, Candles, Dagger, Burned Herbs, Requests on Paper

Gemstones: Red Jasper, Bloodstone, Garnet, Ruby, Quartz Crystals, Carnelian, Tiger's Eye, Rhodochrosite, Agate, Fire Opal, Lava or any volcanic stone such as obsidian or pumace, Metals Gold, Nickle, steel, Brass

Fire Minerals

Looking at the fire at the mineral level, those related to fire are often protective in Nature. They are usually bright and reflective. On color level, they may be red, orange, or yellow in color. Those metals used in forging are sometimes said to correspond with fire, especially if they have been through the forging process. Volcanic stones also tend to be associated with the element of fire.

Fire Herbs

Herbs that correspond with the element of fire tend to cause a warming sensation when smelled, touched, or eaten due to the presence of various chemical constituents or a feeling of pain due to the presence of thorns or spines. They are often protective or anti-inflammatory in nature. Some plants that are traditionally burnt are associated with the element of fire on that basis alone.
- Nettles

- Allspice
- Basil
- Garlic
- Hibiscus
- Juniper,
- Onion (And All Alliums)
- Red Pepper
- Red Poppy
- Thistle
- Almond Tree
- Cacti
- Chile Peppers
- Cinnamon
- Mustard
- Tobacco (Nicotiana)
- Most Nuts
- Seeds And Pods
- Fragrances Clove
- Patchouli
- Bay
- Chamomile

Fire in Dreams

In a dream, Fire can be a purifying element. One can easily relate it to anger, lust, passion, or destruction. Its appearance signifies a significant change is happening.

WICCAN CORRESPONDENCES OF COLORS

Colors have many meanings and properties in Wicca, each color with its own symbolization and connection to other events and happenings in our daily lives. Days, holidays, and even numbers have associations with specific colors.

Since they are all around us, we find them at every turn. Like air, they are tethered to every we encounter. This must have been one of the reasons, human society like colors to various aspects of their lives. Different cultures all around the world each have their own meanings for the different colors, and within these cultures, their meanings have also changed over time.

The ancient Egyptians used colors to represent the powers of their gods. In China, red was not always the most favored color, it was actually yellow. The ancient Mayans, on the other hand, regarded colors as a representation of the ordinal directions north, south, east, and west as well as many different gods in their belief system. Let us now look at the more contemporary meanings of each of the colors and understand their significance in our current cultures.

White

It stands for physical goals, the expulsion of evil spirits, healing, beginning of a new phase, symbolizes purity. Among the ancient Egyptians, white is linked to omnipotence and purity. It shows the sacred power of any god and had always been linked to everything fresh and heavenly. This popular color is used in hospitals as a psyche for quick healing.

Red

It represents a vital source, love, strength, good luck, passion, protection, vitality, fire desire, and fury. It is regarded as one that is of high intensity, on an emotional level. It helps in the stimulation of the senses and has been linked to the increase of the heartbeats and breathes. When people want to warn others, they put up the red warning signs, which depicts 'Danger' or for the people to 'beware.
To showcase pride and strength, mainly during wars or chaos between countries or ancient lands, they use red among their symbols and colors of their flag

Pink

It is the color of love, friendship, harmony, and reconciliation.

Orange

It symbolizes happiness, optimism, successful intention, communication, mental work, career. Often regarded as the healing color, it also shows the luck and warmth of the sun. Many believe that having it around can help in the increase of food. It has helped a lot of people in the stimulation of creativity and enthusiasm.

Brown

It shows protective space, unity with nature, and natural wisdom. This is the color of the earth and shows reliability. It encourages feelings of warmth and security, a sense of secure connection with the universe. In medieval times, brown was associated with the humble lives of the monks, often close to poverty. Today, brown is used in modern interior design to depict something natural, of the earth, warm and living.

Yellow

It stimulates the mind, represents an achievement, learning, happiness, completeness, psychic power. This color is popular in the ancient Chinese as the color of good luck, especially as they often associate with gold. In several parts of the word, yellow is seen as the color of wisdom. When one needs to have his or her optimism, logic, or concentration enhanced, the yellow color can help out. Representing cheerfulness and a free mind of the young, it has also been regarded among the bright, cheerful colors.

Green

It stimulates the brain, denotes prosperity, fertility, love, romance, friendship, harmony. Universally, it is seen as the color that depicts nature and health. It is

linked to newness, growth, money as well as safety.
The god Osiris, represented by green, is regarded as the god of resurrection and fertility. In the middle ages brides were made to wear green because of its symbolization of productivity. Promoting calm, it is the second choice for any hospital or convalescent facilities.

Blue

This is the color of the spirit, healing, idealism, occult protection, wealth. In ancient Egypt, blue is considered as the color of the gods Amon, the god of the wind. They call it the color of oceans and that of the sky. Unlike red, it works towards the evocation of calm and peace as well as tranquility.

It is also linked to people that are loyal, wise, and trustworthy. Seeing blue has a way of spurring the creative part of people into being. It is the color of deep thinking. It has a high psyche on the human mind, and that makes it a perfect color for places created for healings and calmness e.g., hospitals, bedrooms.

Purple

It depicts spiritual strength, purity, healing, psychic work. It is regarded as the color of the nobles and royals. Kings and Queens are shown in the finest when they were purple, that has been mixed with gold. Implying extravagance and sophistication, it also means magic and power.

Black

It is linked to communication with the dead, illustrates the end but also seed to a new beginning, riddance of negativity and negative thoughts. It is connected to death and the underworld but has still been used to symbolize authority and power.

Silver

This is the color of vision and intuition, capacity, purity, healing, psychic work.

Gold

This color represents a great achievement, wealth, durability, integrity, happiness, and mental strength.

DAYS COLORS INCENSE SYMBOLISM

Sunday

Sun orange, white, yellow frankincense, lemon happiness, protection, livelihood, good health, courage, wealth, abundance, spirit strength

Monday

Moon silver, white, grey African violet, myrtle, willow healing, psychic power, spells, inspiration, creativity

Tuesday

Mars red, orange patchouli strong defense, energy, health, debates, lust

Wednesday

Mercury yellow, grey, purple jasmine, lavender communication, exams, travel, meetings, creativity

Thursday

Jupiter blue, magenta, indigo cinnamon, sage, nutmeg, musk abundance, success, happiness, and good health

Friday

Venus green, turquoise, pink sandalwood, saffron, vanilla, strawberry, rose love, friendship, comfort and reconciliation

Saturday

Saturn black, grey, indigo black poppy seeds, myrrh wisdom, freedom from negativity

Major Symbols and the Color That Represent Them

1 – White
2 – Dark blue
3 – Mossy green
4 – Peat brown
5 – Ruby red
6 – Golden yellow
7 – Purple
8 – Orange
9 – Nacre, moon white
10 – Turquoise
11 – Silver
22 – Gold
Earth – Green
Air – Yellow
Fire – Red
Water – Blue
Imbolc – red, pink, brown
Ostara – green, yellow and gold
Beltaine – dark green
Summer Solstice (Litha) – green, blue
Lammas – yellow, orange
Autumn Equinox (Mabon) – orange, brown, yellow

Samhain – black, orange
Yule (Winter Solstice) – red, green, white
Twins – Yellow or silver
Cancer – White
Leo – Yellow or golden
Virgo – Grey
Libra – Pale blue
Scorpio – Black or red
Sagittarius – Blue or purple
Capricorn – Black or dark brown
Aquarius – Blue
Fish – Aquamarine
Aries – Red
Taurus – Green

MAJOR CORRESPONDENCE OF ESSENTIAL OILS

- Anise Star: Bring sacred energies of or beneficence. Used to scent space will drive away and invoke the Gods.
- Basil: Sweet Stimulates the conscious m and is used to clear your mi path to reveal itself. Basil is for crafting and rituals involving
- Bergamot: Increases physical, and mag incre-

ases the flow of mone also help to ensure that you advantage of offers to earn

- Birch Sweet Is used in Rituals involving Workings and invocation of
- Camphor Cleanse and purify your ho negative energies. Used to produce dreams of prophecy
- Carnation Helps to increase your physical energy and is also used in and love.
- Cedarwood Promotes spirituality and d connection with Deity. Ced spell working and Ritual inv
- Cinnamon Leaf Promotes access to psychic visualization to strengthen t in spells to promote wealth.
- Citronella will clear your mind of unwanted energies and will energize y your altar candles with a dr purify and protect your Sacr
- Clary Sage Induces euphoria when in moments. Encourages vividity.
- Clove Leaf Promotes healing and heightened health. Strengthens the conscious retrieving long lost memories
- Cypress Excellent for soothing trauma, particularly the loss of love ending of a relationship. T bestow comfort and solace.
- Dragon's Blood Purification, Ritual magic, l exorcism.
- Eucalyptus Used to heal (purify) a roo psychic energy, primarily engaged in verbal, emotion
- Frankincense Produces a heightened away realms and will deepen any Reduces stress by pointing

bound up with more than one higher consciousness and meditation.
- Ginger Ginger is used in all Rituals Ginger also promotes courage aggression (remember "Har on all levels. Also used to life.
- Grapefruit Pink Used in Rituals involving pr Helps to strengthen your Sp
- Lavender Aids in all Rituals and spell health, love, and peace. Lav depression, and helps to co Sprinkled on your pillow it e
- Lemon Enhances physical energy your Sacred Space or home is also used in healing, or he spells crafting.
- Lemongrass will stimulate and is also used for a person
- Lime Purification and physical en
- Myrrh Awaken's awareness of our everyday existence. Ca questions concerning the fu meditation and healing of t
- Niaouli Useful in overcoming "negative psychic energy intended to scent is invigorating, and pr stimulate our bodies to healthiness
- Nutmeg Physical strength, magickal e awareness, and all spellcraft
- Neroli Purification, joy, and sex.
- Orange Sweet Sweet Orange is ideal for s transforming depression int increase bioelectrical energy workings
- Patchouli can arouse sexual desire energy. Patchouli is also u

WICCA TOOLS FOR BEGINNERS

- Peppermint Will rouse the conscious mi negative thoughts. It can provide purification and visualization all spell and ritual work into invokeCernunnos God, incense, and oil mixtures.
- Pine A very versatile essential oil healing, purification, protect magickal energy and to ma
- Rose Geranium Promotes happiness and pr attacks by calming the bod refreshing it at the same ti psychic attacks and is used, soul.
- Rosemary Used in Rituals and spell cr long life, and happiness. Sn clear your conscious mind memory. Rosemary was Greek temples as an offering and gods.
- Sage White Dalmatian Used to improve memory a conscious mind. With visual used to promote wisdom. Bring money. Do NOT put
- Tea Tree Helps to fight depression a bacterial oil.
- Vanilla, The fragrance of vanilla producing bioelectrical energy, channelled into physical ex rituals. It can also be inhaled sexual relationship.
- Vetivert - Used in folk magic extended protection and money. To the fragrance while visualizing from negative energies. To simmer a few drops in a diff
- Ylang Ylang Aids in all Rituals and spell peace, sex, and love. The fr is soothing and will calm emotional states. With pro be a powerful aphrodisiac.
- Essential Oils by Property

- Addictions: Frankincense
- Aphrodisiac: Amber, Clove (inhaled), Ginger, Lavender, Neroli, Orris Root, Patchouli, Tuberose, Vanilla, Ylang Ylang, Rose, Jasmine
- Attract Customers: Citronella, Sweet Pea
- Attract Friends: Citronella, Sweet Pea
- Awareness: Lavender
- Beauty: Rose
- Birth: Birch, Cyclamen, Jasmine
- Blessings, Spiritual: Frankincense, Sweetgrass, Cypress
- Breaking Curses: Rue, Niaouli
- Breaking Habits: Frankincense
- Business Success: Peony
- Calming: Lavender, Sandalwood, Ylang Ylang
- Change: Peppermint
- Clairvoyance: Cinnamon, Heliotrope, Sandalwood, Anise, Lilac, Saffron
- Cleansing: Jasmine, Pine, Camphor
- Clearing: Sandalwood
- Comfort: Cypress
- Common Sense: Rosemary
- Concentration: Cinnamon
- Confidence: Cedar, Musk, Ginger
- Courage: Musk, Rose Geranium, Clove, Ginger,
- Creativity: Jasmine, Vervain
- Customers Attract: Citronella
- Decisions: Lilac
- Depressant, Anti: Melilot, Clary Sage, Lavender, Sweet Orange, Tea Tree

WICCA TOOLS FOR BEGINNERS

- Determination: All-Spice
- Divination: Anise
- Dreams: Clary Sage
- Ease Childbirth: Cyclamen, Jasmine
- Employment: Ylang Ylang
- Endings: Cypress
- Energy: Vanilla, All-Spice, Bergamot, Carnation, Lemon, Lime, Nutmeg, Pine
- Energy, Restore: Carnation, Vanilla, Patchouli, Vanilla
- Evil, Guard Against Myrrh, Patchouli
- Exorcism: Frankincense, Dragon's Blood
- Eyesight: Clove (inhaled)
- Fear: Myrrh
- Friends, Attract: Citronella
- Focus: Cinnamon
- Guard Against Evil: Myrrh
- Habits, Break: Frankincense
- Happiness: Vanilla, Apple Blossom, Lotus, Basil, Neroli, Rose Geranium, Rosemary
- Harmony: Orange, Rose, Basil, Cumin Seed, Lilac, Magnolia, Narcissus
- Headaches: Lavender
- Healing: Birch, Clove, Eucalyptus, Sandalwood, Lavender, Lotus, Mimosa, Rosemary, Violet, Myrrh, Juniper, Pink Grapefruit, Lemon, Niaouli, Pine, Rose Geranium
- Health: Cinquefoil, Carnation, Lavender, Rose Geranium

- Hex-Breaking: Myrrh
- Higher Consciousness: Wisteria
- Home Luck: Bayberry
- Hope: Sesame
- Illumination: Wisteria
- Insect Repellant: Citronella, vetivert
- Intuition: Honeysuckle
- Invoke Deity: Anise, Birch, Cedar, Peppermint, Rosemary
- Letting Go: Camphor
- Luck: Vanilla
- Luck to the Home: Bayberry
- Love: Apple, Ginger, Jasmine, Rose, Cinquefoil, Coriander, Cyclamen, Gardenia, Lavender, Violet, Carnation, Dragon's Blood, Rosemary, Ylang Ylang
- Longevity: Rosemary
- Magic Ability: Bergamot, Carnation, Dragon's Blood, Lemon, Nutmeg, Sweet Orange, Peppermint, Pine, Rose Geranium, Vanilla
- Marriage: Cyclamen, Orange Blossom, Ylang Ylang
- Meditation: Frankincense, Heliotrope, Acacia, Jasmine, Lotus, Magnolia, Nutmeg, Myrrh, Camphor
- Memory: Clove, Lilac, Honeysuckle, Rosemary, Sage
- Mental Ability: Rosemary, Clove
- Money: Bayberry, Cinquefoil, Ginger, Hyssop, Patchouli, Basil, Bergamot, Cinnamon, Nutmeg, Pine, Sage, Vetivert

WICCA TOOLS FOR BEGINNERS

- Moon: Birch
- Negativity-Anti: Rue, Anise Star, Citronella, Niaouli, Peppermint, Vetivert, Ylang Ylang
- Originality: Jasmine
- Passion: Musk, Ginger
- Peace: Lavender, Myrrh, Rose, Cumin Seed, Lilac, Magnolia, Narcissus, Rose, Tuberose, Basil, Jasmine, Ylang Ylang
- Peace of Mind: Apple, Benzoin, Hyacinth, Patchouli
- Permanence: Lavender
- Power: Orange, Carnation, Cinquefoil
- Prophetic Dreams: Mimosa
- Prosperity: Honeysuckle, Almond, Bergamot (when oil is worn in the palm of each hand), Lotus, Mint (anoint wallet), Peony, Vervain
- Protection: Anise, Bergamot, Cinnamon, Clove, Dragon's Blood, Frankincense, Heliotrope, Jasmine, Sandalwood, Cinquefoil, Cedar, Gardenia, Myrrh, Nutmeg, Rose Geranium, Rosemary, Rue, Juniper, Pink Grapefruit, Niaouli, Pine, Vetivert
- Protection from Misery: Cedar
- Protection from Misfortune: Cedar
- Protective Spirits: Lemon
- Prudence: Rosemary
- Psychic Ability: Acacia, Camphor, Lemon Grass, Magnolia, Tuberose, Cinnamon, Lemongrass, Nutmeg
- Purification: Dragon's Blood, Frankincense,

Benzoin, Eucalyptus, Hyssop, Lavender, Musk, Myrrh, Juniper, Camphor, Citronella, Lemongrass, Lime, Neroli, Sweet Orange, Peppermint, Pine
- Quick-Thinking: Honeysuckle, Basil, Citronella
- Relaxation: Apple, Lavender, Apple Blossom, Hyacinth, Jasmine, Narcissus, Peppermint
- Restore Energy: Carnation, Vanilla
- Sacred Space: Anise, Citronella, Eucalyptus, Lemon
- Self-Assurance: Musk, Rosemary
- Self-Control: Cedar
- Sex: Ginger, Neroli, Patchouli, Vanilla, Ylang Ylang
- Sleep: Jasmine, Nutmeg, Lavender
- Sorrow: Myrrh
- Spirits, Protective: Lemon
- Spiritual Blessings: Frankincense, Sweetgrass
- Spirituality: Cinnamon, Lilac, Heliotrope, Jasmine, Myrrh, Frankincense,
- Stability: Lavender
- Strength: Musk, Cinquefoil, Cinnamon, Pink Grapefruit
- Stress: Lavender, Frankincense
- Success: Apple Blossom, Ginger
- Success, Business: Peony
- Sympathy: Basil
- Tranquillity: Rose
- Transformation: Sweetgrass, Sweet Orange
- Transitions: Cypress
- Understanding: Honeysuckle, Myrrh

- Vitality: All-Spice, Rosemary, Vanilla
- Wisdom: Apple, Cinquefoil, Sage

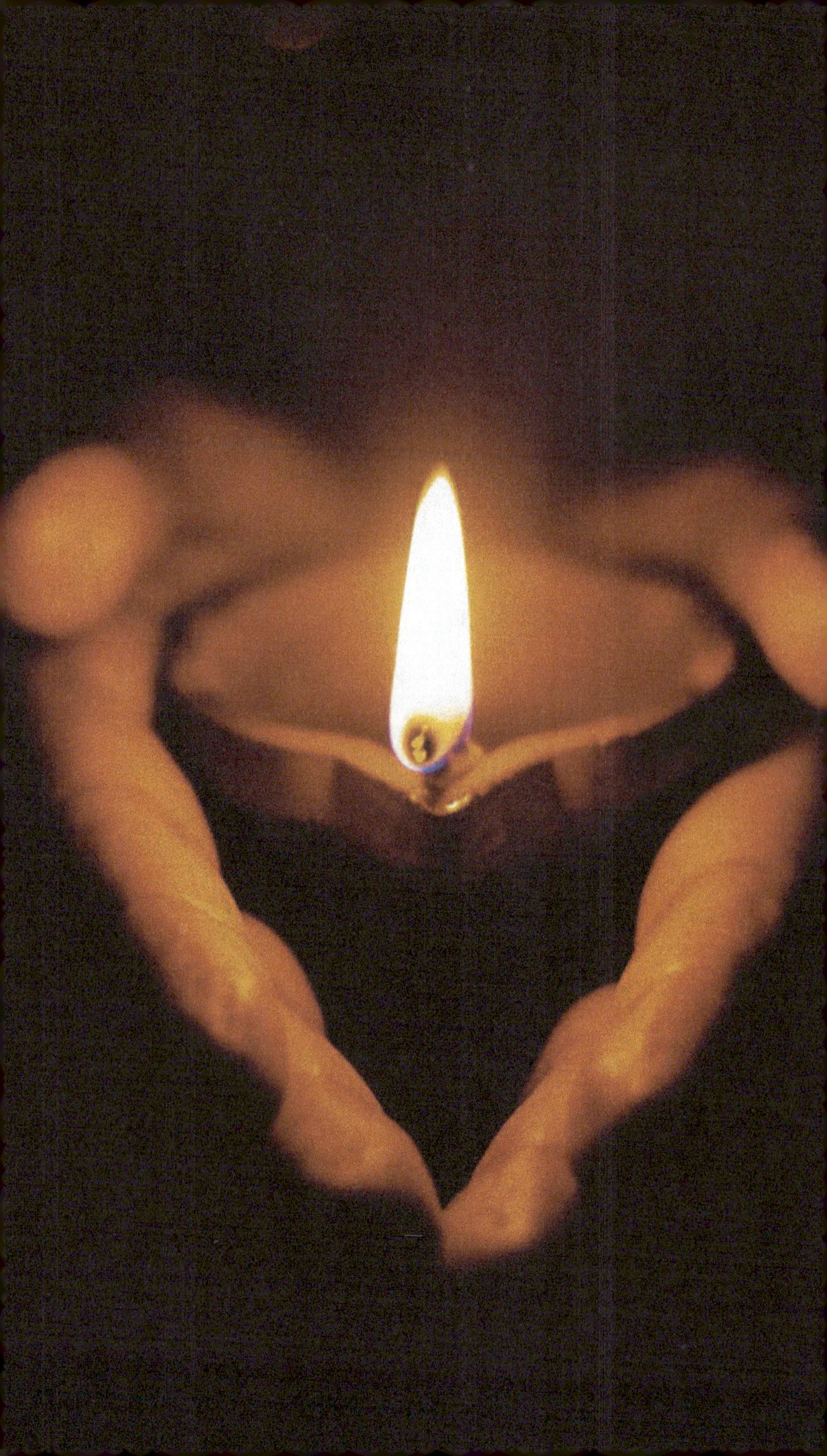

CHAPTER - 4
Simple spells you can cast

Casting simple spells are easy. As much as you have to study hard for the actualization of reality, you still need to follow the due process by using the spells others have successfully tried.

A WICCAN LOVE SPELL

With this Wiccan love spell, you can send a beam of love to someone. It is something they will feel subconsciously without their free will being affected. All it does is purify the energetic connection between the two of you, like clearing up the pathway for the spiritual connection. But nobody's free will be compromised.

Timing

Wait until nighttime to cast this spell. A Friday is best for casting love spells. A full moon is also great for increasing the power of the spell.

The Spell Casting

> "MY HEART ABLAZE AND SHINING, THIS LOVE I DO SEND TO THEE, IF YOU FIND A PLACE IN YOUR HEART TO LOVE ME, BY THE GREATEST GOOD, SO MOTE IT BE."

PROTECTION SPELL FOR YOU

You can also create your own protection spell! Magic is most potent when you follow your own intuition, so as long as you educate yourself and take great care and attention, you can write your own spells.

- Set your intention: Begin by setting your goal. What is your purpose? In this case, you aim to get a protective spell.
- Write your spell: Next, write down the spell. It can be short and to the point or long and poetic. What matters is the intention behind it and the honesty.
- Gather supplies: Take the time to collect all of your magical supplies. Whether you will be using colored candles, crystals, herbs, or oils, be sure to have everything at hand before you begin.
- Time your spell: choose a time where you won't be disturbed and use the power of the moon properly.

- Cast the circle: invoke each direction and element to aid you in your work.
- Send the intention: visualize and send your energy into the universe.
- Close the circle and give thanks: always thank any God or Goddess that may have helped you in your work. Close the circle by reversing the original casting. Say,

> "I THANK YOU AND RELEASE YOU.".

EASY WICCAN LUCK SPELL

This is a beginner luck spell that is very safe to perform. Don't worry about negative consequences with this one. It will give your life the extra push it, and you can use it to boost your luck on anything you are trying to accomplish in your life

Timing

Cast this spell during the waxing or moon, when there is an abundance of energy.
Spellcasting:

God and goddess spirits and guides, that all that I have. I ask you now for [insert want].
Aid me as I work to achieve this bring it to me when

the time is right.
 So Fire, ignite my dream for the highest
Seal my dream for the highest go

**Don't forget, this spell may bring you luck in unexpected ways, so remain open-minded. Success will always manifest for the highest go your right path. Keep your eyes open for opportunities and perhaps surprising abundance.

> YOU CAN FIND MORE AND MORE SPELLS ON THE BOOK "WICCA ALTAR FOR BEGINNERS"
> (THE GREEN BOOK)
> CHECK IT OUT ON AMAZON.

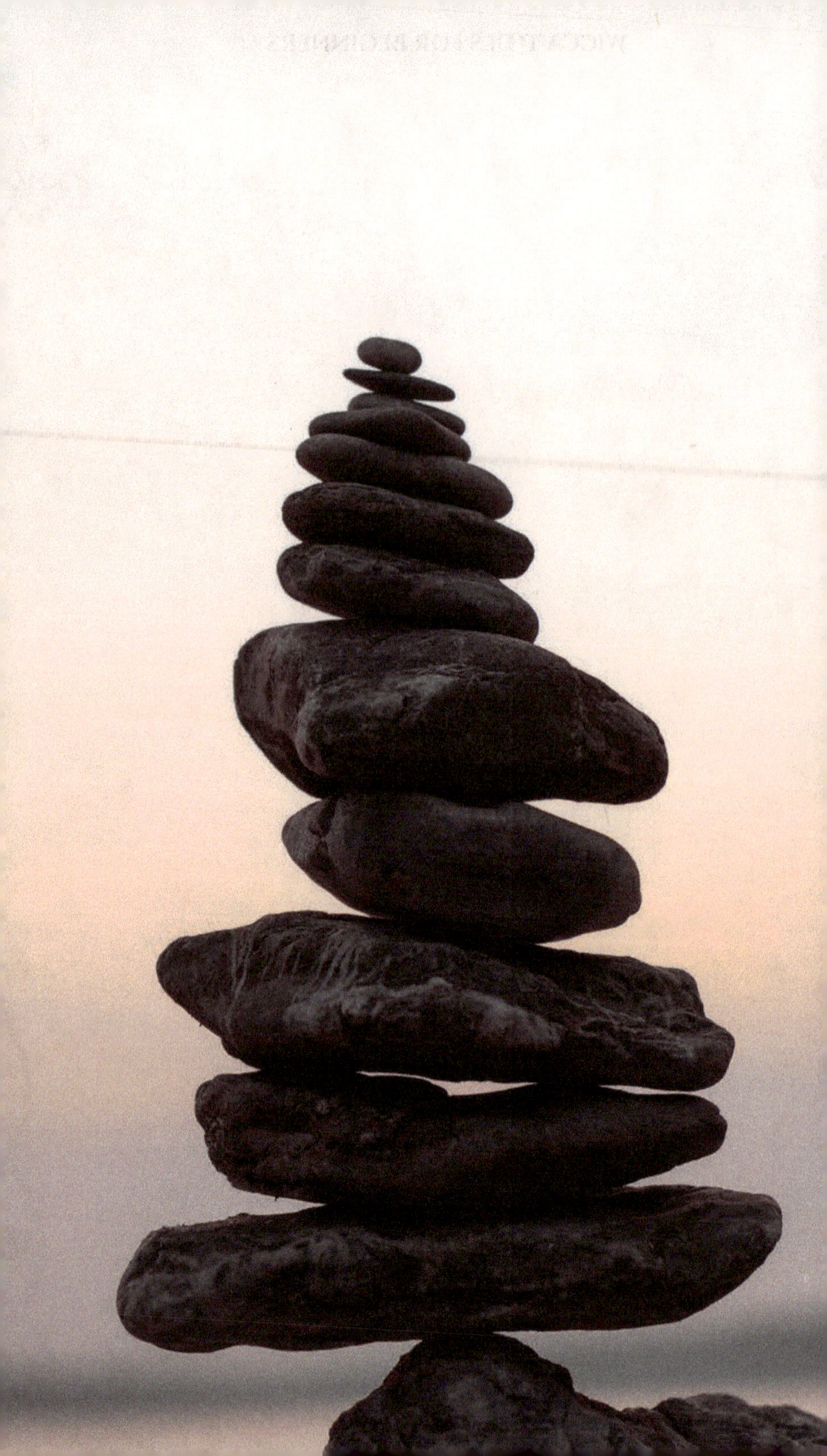

CHAPTER - 5
How to use the wicca to Self Help and Sefl Care

Self-care is a necessary activity that every witch or Wiccan practitioner needs to practice. The self- care ensures that the individual is a proper state of mind and is mentally able to handle any mental activity.

The world is unarguable a harsh place to live in. as such, it is important to stay safe from every unnecessary evil and attack. Protecting yourself from the evil that has plagued the world is of utmost importance. This implies that you disconnect yourself from every evil or negative force that may affect everything positive you represent.

Furthermore, the Wicca spells and rituals can also help the practitioner create a deeper bond with him/herself. it also brings about inner peace and balance for the individual who practices self -help with Wicca.

Self-care entails remembering every minute detail that concerns you and all your related activity. With the aid of magic, it is easier to get things done and remember information that is necessary for your improvement and development. One notable feature of the Wiccan practice to self- help or care is that it enables the practitioners to create their individual mantra.

Wiccans maximize the use of self- help to maximize their life and get the very best out of it. As a matter of fact, the Wicca practice and self- care are entwined. One cannot do without the other.

The various ways of using Wicca for self- help/care are:

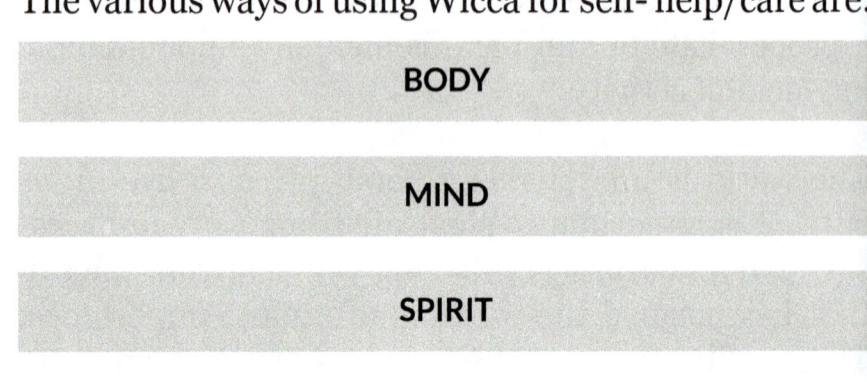

BODY

MIND

SPIRIT

THE BODY

The Wicca practice ascribes much importance to the body. The religion recognizes that the body plays a very important role in the existence of man. It refers to the body as a temple. As such, Wicca practitioners are of the liberty to safeguard the body from every unnecessary attacks and activity that would affect the body and how it functions. Some Wicca practitioners succumb to decorating their bodies with everything they feel is appropriate to beautify their temple. Some of these things include the use of tattoo to beautify the body, wearing makeup and making use of hair dyes. All of these are used by a Wicca practitioner if they feel it would enhance their bodily appearance. However, there are also healthy choices that are made as regarding what should be consumed by the mouth. Wiccan practitioners take special care to monitor the foods that go into their bodies.

It is a wise thing to always be careful about what goes into the mouth and the type of medication to be taken. Wicca practitioners are of the opinion that certain medication will affect their bodies and how it functions. There is however no rule to this as long as you eat what you feel is appropriate for your body and will not affect your temple.

Some practitioners of Wicca argue that they cannot eat any food that comes from the ground but would rather settle for foods that come from the womb. In this way, you will be at liberty to avoid the chances of eating processed foods. Though, some practitioners that eat such meals state that it helps them to stay healthy at all times.

Hence, when you stay away from harmful food substances, it keeps you safe from unnecessary weight gain and any health-related ailment. In this way, it is best for you to eat fruits and vegetables. Fruits, vegetables, and proteins keep your body in a working condition and make you fit to engage in any activity. Eating appropriate meals demonstrates the kind of love you have for your health and body.

Additionally, it is also necessary to exercise the body at all times. Exercising the body keeps it fit at all times and prevents your susceptibility to infections and health issues. When your body is adequately exercised, and you also take care of your body by eating good foods there are higher chances of getting the needed energy for spells.

The body is a very important part of every Wiccan ritual and spells to be active. This is because the body is actively involved in the physical part of the process. The chants, movements, and rituals are only performed with the physical part of the body. So, it is essential to take adequate care of the body. Additionally, the energy that is required to carry out a spell or ritual successfully is only gotten from the body.

More so, you can make use of the beauty of nature. Wicca makes use of natural items and elements for a spell to be activated. The love for nature is held in high esteem in the Wicca religion. Whenever you can, enjoy nature and revel in its beauty. Take a walk in the garden and appreciate natural elements. This is just another way to care for your body. As a Wiccan practitioner, different elements are at play to ensure the success of every activity or spell that you carry out. Without the elements in total cooperation, the spell may not be activated. As a Wiccan practitioner, nature is another beautified opportunity of being in the presence of gods and goddesses. They are available in these natural elements. You may not be able to see them with the eyes, but it doesn't take away the fact that they are present in the elements. If you want to feel the heightened presence of divine beings, give your body a treat and spend quality time in nature. Admire the stones, precious metals, sun, moon, stars and so on. These elements are the right way for you to appreciate the supremacy of the various gods and goddesses.

THE MIND

The mind is a weapon that can either make or mar a man. Whatever a man chooses to be stay from the position of the mind. This destructive tool can also be used to generate something very beautiful and desirable. With Wicca, it is possible to make use of the mind to call forth a lot of attractive blessings and beautiful things around you. The mind is used for meditation purposes. It is easy to stay connected to the gods and goddesses through meditation. Meditation cleanses the mind from unwanted negative energy and helps it to stay focus at all times. It helps you to focus on the right practice for casting a spell. With the use of meditation, it is possible for the practitioner to cast a spell and it would come out successful. Meditation also helps to promote the right choices and attitudes that are needed for all-round development. The choices that you make stem from your mind. The extent to which you achieve certain things in life is determined by the state of your mind. So, let the mind become a constructive weapon that would aid to shape your life and bring forth something positive from it.

There are bound to be times when you may not understand the right way to go about certain situations, meditation comes in handy in such situations. There are cases of a practitioner enduring an abusive marriage because of societal pressures and expectations. The moment she realized that the marriage was not benefiting her in the right kind of way, she left the relationship and now she is living her best life. This can also be you if you accept the opportunity to make your life beautiful and colorful. You can choose to make meditation a habit in your daily life. This is a healthy plan for your mind. All that you require is the ability to concentrate on a certain positive aspect of your life and discard the others that threaten your peace of mind.

THE SPIRIT

Is it possible to discuss results without the place of the spirit? The spirit is the ideal representation of man. The body may die someday and cease to exist, but this is never the case with the spirit. The spirit never dies. More so, the only way to stay connected in performing a ritual is to make use of the spirit. Thus, the spirit must be actively involved in any ritual to come out successful. It is almost impossible to achieve the desired results without the place of the spirit. Hence, whenever a ritual is performed, you are privileged to evolve spiritually. At the point of any ritual, you are no longer the person you used to be before the ritual commenced but a spirit- fill individual.

Whenever you perform a ritual, you are not only involved in physical activity but a spiritual filled activity. You may not realize it, but magic is a lot more spiritual than physical. How? There are a lot of forces that are present for the spell to be activated. The ritual creates a magnifying transformation within the core of your spirit. How do you care for your spirit? This is a very simple answer, yet the question plagues a lot of hearts including yours, right? Well, not too worry, I have the answer that you seek. You can take care of your spirit by ensuring that the spirit is involved in a lot of spiritual exercises. You need to accept the fact that just like the body is a physical structure that is fed with physical substances, the spirit is a spiritual being that needs to be kept active with the sue of spiritual substances.

WICCA TOOLS FOR BEGINNERS

These spiritual substances include spiritual activities such as performing rituals, castings spells, and meditation. All of these are spiritually related activity and to keep the spirit in the appropriate state all of these should be encouraged.

These spiritual activities help you to stay connected to the divine beings and enlighten your spiritual understanding of spiritual matters. It helps you to learn more about life and all activities that surround life. This makes it easier for you to address certain issues that need adequate attention. More so, you will be entitled to learn certain life lessons. The gods and goddesses also help you become a better person through the communication you make with them. Your spirit also becomes lifted when you are connected through the Wiccan ritual. With the aid of Wiccan practice, you are able to maintain a level of consciousness that would aid you to become better at the things that you do. As long as your spirit is connected, the divine forces help you to get the answer you seek.

All of this is important in the Wiccan practice as it helps you to stay in good shape and makes you healthy. Self- care helps you to maximize your potential as a practitioner and get the very best out of your life.

THE STEPS TO ACHIEVING YOUR SELF-CARE ROUTINES

The first step is to relax

You need to relax your mind. You cannot have proper coordination of your body, spirit and, mind if you don't relax your nerves. You do not need a whole lot of activities in your daily life. When you pay too much attention to the situations around you, it could hinder you from performing properly at the activities you get involved with. It is important you favor lots of self- caring practices that would aid you to relax your mind. Your spirit, mind, and body function properly together. None can work well without the other. It is unfair on yourself if you get too engrossed in different activities and then you lose yourself and focus in pursuit of all those factors. To achieve desired intentions and to promote your self- care, you need to understand what self- care entails and be the best version of yourself.

Love yourself

You need to love yourself enough to care for yourself. If you do not love and respect yourself, you will never be able to be all that you want to be. it is only when you appreciate yourself that you can confidently accept everything that concerns you and be the best person for yourself. Loving yourself recognizes the place of growth. It comes with an understanding of your imperfections alongside a desire to be better than you were yesterday. When you love yourself, you become aware of everything you need for your mind, body, and spirit to grow. None of this would be realistic if you don't love yourself enough. It is only when you love yourself that you would begin to pay attention to the different factors that are responsible for your growth and success.

Don't succumb to every distraction that comes your way

This is a benefit of meditation. Meditation helps you to become better and takes away every possibility of undue circumstances and pressures from your path.

This may sound funny, but it is very important. The only person that can stop you from being all you need to be is you. This is usually the case with a lot of practitioners. Sometimes, some of the negative forces we fight actually come from you. You may be a problem with the ability to become better. How? The place of ego! Ego prevents you from achieving everything you hope to achieve. It stems from your being and pins you down to a spot where you can neither grow nor move. This is a very worrisome situation for a majority of people. So, to change this mentality and problem, you need to learn how to care for yourself and do away with everything that contradicts your being and ability to grow. If you do not have the ability to trust yourself, how would you trust everything around you? Ego and doubt make it difficult for you to forge ahead and achieve all you hope to get from life. It will limit you in all ramifications. So, if you sincerely desire to care for your totality, you need to start by appreciating everything about it.

WICCA TOOLS FOR BEGINNERS

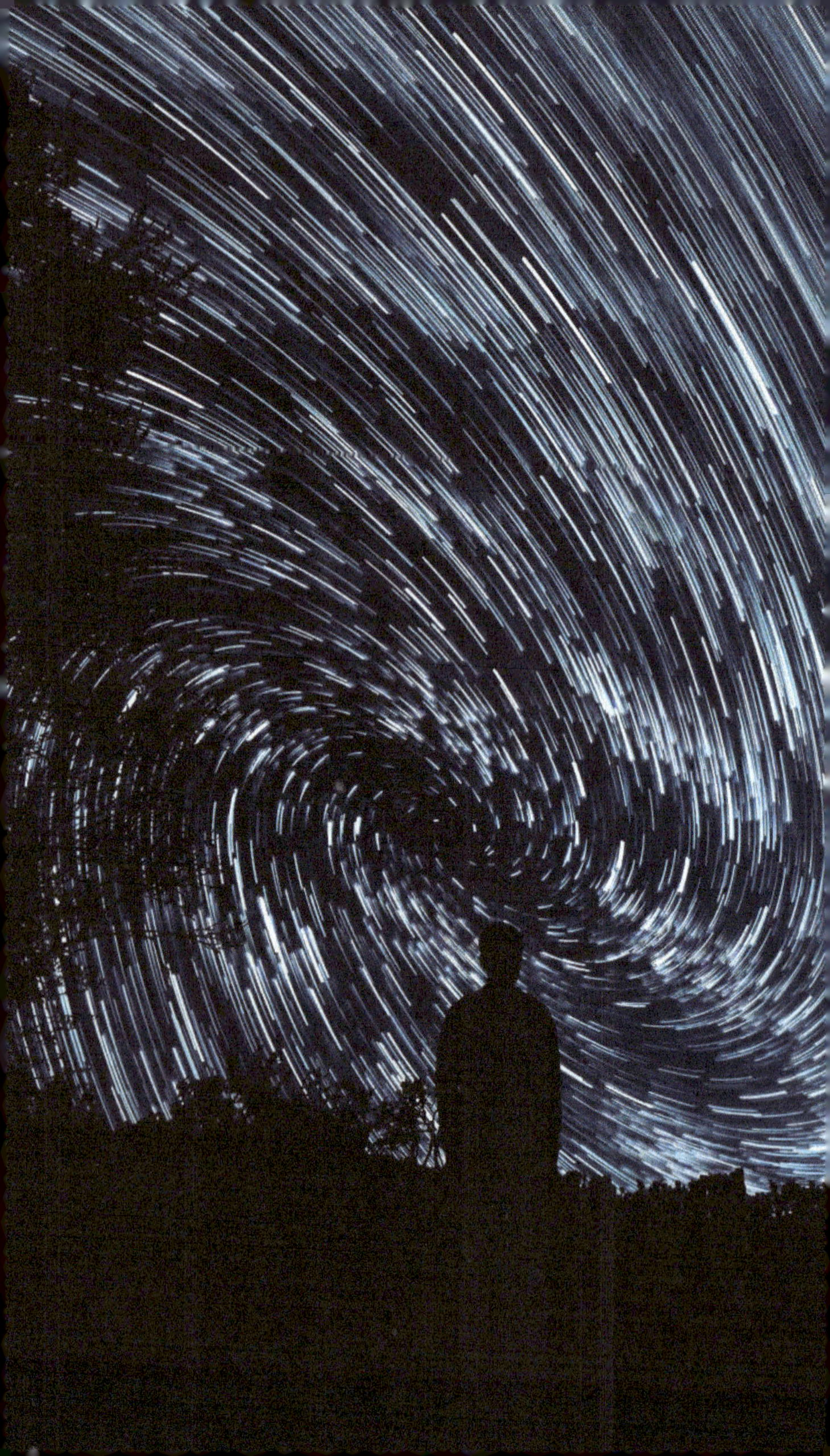

CHAPTER - 6
A bit of astrology

In Wiccan practice, astrology is entwined with your birth month. It is believed that every birth month has a zodiac sign and this zodiac sign ensures that the practitioner can rely on its efficiency to get the best result from practicing the religion.

The astrology in Wiccan involves different factors that play a unifying part to ensure that everything works in your favor. The various forces are the sun, moon, elements, and planets. Fortunately, all of these parts are natural things that help to ensure that you get the best from your birth month.

An understanding of the forces in your birth month and how to combine them effectively will help you to get the results from every spell or magic you cast.

The sun is a natural element that helps you understand how you cat in a certain condition; that is in an extroverted situation. The moon sign is an opposing force to the sun. unlike the sun that unveils how you react to extroverted situations; the moon helps to reveal how you act in your "alone" time. whatever you find yourself doing at any of these times is a born of your astrological signs.

However, there are other signs that aids you know more about your astrological signs. The planet type also makes it possible for you to understand the external forces that you interact with. In cases where you feel your human mind is influenced or affected, you will understand the factors that are at play with the aid of your astrological sign.

It is, therefore, necessary to come to terms with the reality that your astrological sign constitutes a major part of your life. You need to act on the forces that are at play in your astrological life to bring forth the desired result you aim for. Though, this doesn't mean that your astrological sign determines your goal in life. It doesn't define your goal or life aspirations. It only helps to give you an understanding of your reality. Everyone needs a balance to achieve their aims and goals in life. Your astrological signs create the desired balance that would prepare you to be the individual you hope to be.

The astrology of Wicca reminds you of who you are and how you can be better. It is a reminder of your originality and prepares you to be the best version of yourself. It makes it easier for you to accommodate. A typical instance is when you notice you are being overly erratic to certain conditions. It doesn't mean you are not normal. It is simply your astrological elements acting in the direction of your sign. Except you realize that it doesn't totally define who you are, you may not get the right kind of understanding that would help you to become better. The astrological sign also creates room for change. If you are not in total support of any of your behavioral patterns, you are at liberty to change. The astrological sign of Wicca does not mitigate change. It encourages change that can bring positive development in the life of the practitioner. But, if you bring bad change upon yourself, you only have yourself to blame. So, act accordingly. Do what is best for you and would cause you to be better than you were yesterday.

Wicca religion takes the astrological signs very seriously. Just like the various elements play a significant role in performing rituals and casting spells. So, it is linked with astrological importance. Wiccan religion attaches a lot of significance and importance to the different signs and elements. Astrology in Wicca is used to refer to a lot of factors such as the zodiac signs. The zodiac signs as well refer to various natural elements like air, water, and earth. It also refers to a different gender, plenary leadership and a host of others.

It is very important that a Wiccan practitioner know their respective signs. It is beneficial when you want to cast a spell. In casting a spell, you can make use of your zodiac sign to make it more effective and to turn out successful. The astrological signs differ from one person to the next. The signs represent different individuals' personalities and attributes.

THE NATURAL ELEMENTS AND WHAT THEY REPRESENT

Water

This is an important natural element. A lot of factors are held together by this element. So many times, water has been regarded or ascribed to life. It shows that the role that this element plays is very large and causes a great impact on the lives of many people. Water is basically found in a lot of places and too many people rely on the source of water for many varying needs. So, water is an element that can be used to bring up something good.

Individuals in this category are usually emotional beings. They find it easy to associate with people but do not have the right words to say to anyone. Their feelings are always intact, but they lack the ability to convey their emotions and words when need be.

The various people that possess the water element are the zodiac signs of Scorpio, Pisces, and cancer. People in this category are regarded to be the strongest individuals in terms of emotional traits.

Earth

This is not just the physical part of the world. In Wiccan, it goes beyond the solid part of the world people walk on. The Earth element represents individuals who are stubborn in their ways, realistic and also stable. Hence, there are three categories of individuals in the Earth element.

Individuals in the earth element are very realistic in their approach towards life. They attend to situations the way it seems and don't pay attention to unimportant details about the world. Their emotions are also stable as they can make decisions that affect t their personalities and their lives without a flinching thought. People in the earth element do not accept ideas that seem conflicting especially with their own ideas. They have a mind of theirs and tend to act in that regard.

The zodiac signs that belong to the earth element are Capricorn, Virgo, and Taurus. They perceive the world from a realistic point of view and try their best to avoid being biased.

Fire

This is not the physical representation of the element. Though, the physical representation of the element also reflects in its natural form. The individuals in this category are considered very lively and interesting to be with. The fire element comprises of individuals who are insensitive to the plight of the people around them. But, just like its physical representation, they light up the lives of people they encounter. They are also high-spirited individuals and it always exudes in their personalities. The zodiac signs in this element are Leo, Aries, and Sagittarius. These individuals in this category are regarded as action-packed, spirit- fill and adequately vitalized personalities.

Air

The last but not the least element. Is it possible to do anything without the aid of air? Every individual need air to survive and to cope with life and all that there is to life. The individuals in this element are considered to be very analytical and approach situations adequately. They also have very good ideas and can bring forth something good and beneficial from the use of their ideas. as a matter of fact, they look at things in a rational manner. But, one shortcoming about this element is that they actually do not do well in handling their emotions. Their emotions can get the better part of them and this may be their undoing. They experience a lot of issues in dealing with their emotions and how they feel about people.

The zodiac sign in this category is Gemini, Aquarius, and Libra.

It is very necessary to understand the strengths and weaknesses of the various elements. An understanding of this factor makes it easy for you to get the best from your astrological signs. More so, you will understand how to tap into the potency of your element and how to use it to your best ability.

THE DIFFERENT QUALITIES OF THE ZODIAC SIGNS

It doesn't only stop at knowing your zodiac signs. You have a responsibility to9 find out the mode the different zodiac sign belongs to. The understanding of the various mode of the zodiac sign will help your element to mature into the right phase and hence you can actually use to your benefit.

There are three modes. They are the fixed, cardinal and mutable mode.

The fixed category

This kind of mode is usually dominated by the zodiac signs of Scorpio, Leo, Aquarius, and Taurus. The individuals that possess the fixed mode are known as being obstinate and unwilling to accept a change. Their opinions are sometimes fixed, and they do not appreciate the concerns or plights of others.

They represent the initial phase of any season. The people in this category are not easily discouraged from doing whatever they set out to do. They are neither discouraged by their inadequacies or incapabilities to accept their flaws. Even when they are not capable of carrying out an activity, they are still willing to give it a try nonetheless.

The fixed mode may not have the ability to successfully beginning a project, but they lack the ability to push through with the project. So, when others feel that they won't be able to carry on, the fixed mode always finds a way to push through with the task. They believe in paying attention to ways they can gather energies towards achieving the desired goal.

The cardinal category

The individuals in this category experience little difficulty in starting up projects. They find it easy to begin a task, but the major issue lies in actually completing the task that they have set out to accomplish. Thus, they are perfect beginners but bad finishers. Though, this is not entirely true for all of them. Just like the name hints, the cardinal mode addresses the four major cardinal points of the zodiac signs. The initial phase of every season, equinoxes and the solstice points. This is very important in the cardinal category and should not be taken for granted. hence, it is important to have the right idea and information on the cardinal mode.
The zodiac sign in this category includes cancer, Libra, Aries, and Capricorn.

The mutable category

The individuals in this category are referred to as being very considerate about the plight of people around them. They show great concern to the issues that affect people around them.
This sign is often perceived to be the most common type of sign. They are actually very common, and they include the zodiac sign such as Gemini, Pisces, Sagarittus, and Virgo. These signs are notable for an extraordinary relationship with people around them and

would do anything possible to avert a situation that would cause uneasiness for the concerned individual. If you find yourself caring deeply about an individual and how they feel at all times. Then, the chances are that you belong to the mutable mode.

Various genders

Just like the Wiccan religion recognizes the place of gods and goddesses, the same applies to gender. In Wiccan religion, various signs are used to symbolize either male or female gender. In performing a ritual, it is necessary to pay attention to the sex of the sign. It aids to increase the potency of the ritual. This fact should not be taken for granted.
Examples of the masculine sign are the Gemini zodiac sign, Libra zodiac sign, Leo zodiac sign, Aquarius sign, and Sagarittus zodiac sign.
Examples of the feminine sign of astrology are the Pisces zodiac sign, Scorpio zodiac sign, Cancer zodiac sign, Virgo zodiac sign, Taurus zodiac sign, and Capricorn zodiac sign.
One factor that mitigates against the place of the gender sign is that almost all practitioners perceive the signs to be the same. So, it becomes difficult to associating one sign as being feminine or masculine.

The planets

The planets are another important part of astrology in the Wiccan religion. That is the major reason some spells are cast only when the sun or moon is at its peak.

This is so because the Wiccan religion takes this element into consideration.

The twelve various signs are entwined with a planet. So, it is important to know about your own sign and its planet. One notable characteristic of the planet is that it shares similar qualities with the sign it represents. Though, there will always be some differences between the planet and the sign it represents. A huge difference is that the planet is capable of moving around from one place to the next, but the signs do not move around rather they are an attribute of a personality. All of this is important in Wiccan practice. Take note of the differences and act accordingly.

THE ATTRIBUTES OF EACH SIGN

Libra

The Libra zodiac sign is a masculine gender with medicinal astrology of kidneys and adrenals. Scales are a symbolic part of the Libra sign. The oils that can be used by this zodiac sign are black pepper, frankincense, basil, and Melissa. It has a cardinal based quality with its planet type as Venus. It belongs to the element of air. The permissible magic with this zodiac sign is the magic or ritual that is related to relationships, art, social-based activities and magic related to justice.

Virgo

This zodiac sign is considered a feminine gender with medicinal astrology of stomach and bowels. Virgin is a symbolic part of the Virgo sign. The oils that can be lemon, grapefruit, thyme, and ginger. It has a mutable based quality with its planet type as mercury. It belongs to the element of the earth. The permissible magic with this zodiac sign is the magic or ritual that is related to health and domestic-related concerns.

Cancer

This Zodiac sign is considered a feminine gender with medicinal astrology of breast and cancer. Crab is a symbolic part of the Cancer sign. The oils that can be used by this zodiac sign are ginger, rosemary, lavender, and juniper. It has a cardinal based quality with its planet type as the moon. It belongs to the element of the water. The permissible magic with this zodiac sign is the magic or ritual that is related to fertility and protection.

Sagarittus

This zodiac sign is considered a masculine gender with medicinal astrology of thighs and hips. Archer is a symbolic part of the Sagarittus sign. The oils that can be used tea tree, rosemary, and frankincense. It has a mutable based quality with its planet type as Jupiter. It belongs to the element of the fire.
This zodiac sign is usually notable for various activi-

ties such as religion, philosophy, education, and languages.

Leo

This zodiac sign is considered a masculine gender with medicinal astrology of heart. The Lion is a symbolic part of the Leo sign. The oils that can be used garlic, rosemary, and lemon. It has a fixed based quality with the planet type as the sun. it belongs to the element of the fire.

This zodiac sign is usually notable for various attributes like self- confidence, success, and drama

Scorpio

This zodiac sign is considered a feminine gender with the medicinal astrology of the sex parts. Scorpio is a symbolic part of the Scorpio sign. The oils that can be used are sandalwood and jasmine. It has a fixed based quality with the planet type as the Pluto. It belongs to the element of water.

The scorpion sign possesses the attributes the death, power, and obsession.

Capricorn

This zodiac sign is considered a feminine gender with the medicinal astrology of the knees and bones. Goat is a symbolic part of the Scorpio sign. The oils that can be used are tea, ginger, and eucalyptus. It has a cardinal based quality with the planet type as the Saturn. It

belongs to the element of water.
Capricorn is essential in achieving whatever one hopes to achieve. Additionally, it also favors traditional activities and nostalgia.

Pisces

This zodiac sign is considered a feminine gender with the medicinal astrology of the feet. Fish is a symbolic part of the Pisces sign. The oils that can be used are lavender and sandalwood. It has a mutable based quality with the planet type as Neptune. It belongs to the element of water.
Pisces possess the following attributes of compassion, imagination, and creativity.

Aquarius

This zodiac sign is considered a masculine gender with the medicinal astrology of the ankles and calves. Water-bearer is a symbolic part of the Aquarius sign. The oils are peppermint, lemon, and rose. It has fixed based quality with the planet type as Uranus.it belongs to the element of air.
Aquarius reveals attributes such as innovation, invention, and inspiration.

Aries

This zodiac sign is considered a masculine gender with the medicinal astrology of the head. Ram is a symbolic part of the Aquarius sign. The oils are black pepper, lemon, and rosemary. It has a cardinal based quality with the planet type as Mars. It belongs to the element of air.

Taurus

This zodiac sign is considered a feminine gender with medicinal astrology of the throat. The bull is a symbolic part of the Taurus sign. The oils are rosemary, lemon, and rose. It has a fixed based quality with the planet type as Venus. It belongs to the element of Air.

Gemini

This zodiac sign is considered a masculine gender with medicinal astrology of the arms. Twins are a symbolic part of the Gemini sign. The oils are grapefruit, ginger, and basil. It has a mutable based quality with the planet type as Mercury. It belongs to the element of air.

The significance of the various twelve astrology signs is to ensure that a suitable ritual is performed by the concerned individual. Every ritual or sign is dependent on the proper steps of carrying out such a ritual. If you are desirous of getting optimum results from any ritual or spell you carry out, make sure you are knowledgeable about your astrological sign. As a Wiccan practitioner, it is of utmost importance to recognize what works best for your sign and stick to it for an effective result.

EXAMPLES OF THE VARIOUS SIGNS AND ITS INTERPRETATION

If your rising sign is in 07 degrees Virgo

This is actually a prevalent sign with a lot of people. Do not be panicky. It isn't totally bad for you.

The individuals with this sign are shy and are not assertive. They doubt their self-esteem and do not have the required confidence to effectively socialize with people. They feel inadequate in their interaction with people. Sometimes, they think they are not interesting to be with and are not smart for people to communicate with. But in reality, the set of individuals with this sign are usually friendly and soft-spoken. They are very orderly and take cleanliness quite seriously. Other type of individuals admires them a lot for their qualities.

Perfectionism is the quality of the people with this sign. They are very practical and are equipped with the natural will- power to address people in a tactful condition. They identify the fault and address it without mincing words. However, they are keen to offer their assistance whenever the need arises. They pay special attention to their appearance and are always bent on appearing graceful at all times. They are very sensible and have zero tolerance for indiscipline and other related negative virtues. They pay attention to delivering the result as such they do their best in their work environment.

If the sun is in 09 degrees Aquarius

Individuals with this sign are receptive to new ideas and information. They are ever willing to learn and do not appreciate a particular status quo. Change is their watchword. They are free-spirited individuals and are appreciative of friends. In as much as they love keeping friends, they do not enjoy feeling overburdened by constant emotion demands from the extended arms of friendship. This implies that whenever they feel that their friendship with you is about to have an emotional effect on them, they are quick to withdraw from you.
Change doesn't come easy to this sign. Such persons would prefer to stick to what they are comfortable with than to accept a change. They are also very stubborn individuals and are sometimes insensitive to the needs of others. They do not pay attention to the needs of others and can also effectively lead a group of people. The individuals in this sign are very observant of the situations around them. They are also objective in making their decisions. Most individuals in this sign group are suitable to offer courses like computer science or astrology.

If the moon is in 28-degrees Scorpio

The individuals in this sign happen to be too emotional in whatever they feel. If they are angry or happy, they tend to over-exaggerate the emotion. They have intense emotional displays. The emotions they exhibit are usually considered not appropriate by people around them. Sometimes, they also find it difficult to understand how they behave or express their emotions. Emotionally, they are very unstable and would rather settle for the uncertainties associated with their sign irrespective of the consequences of the emotional outburst. They are either too jealous of others or doubt themselves. In other words, the individuals in this sign, suffer from inferiority complex and would rather depend on others to reassure them of their true worth or standard. They have a curious mind and want to find out about the things that happen around them. They would make great detectives if they choose to. They hope to find out more about human emotions and nature. Nonetheless, individuals with this sign are advised to be considered in their actions and attitude towards people. If not, they will meet such opposition form the people they also associate with.

If mercury is in 19 degrees Aquarius

They are opinionated minded individuals. They have a way with words and as such, they are comfortable expressing themselves and actions to the people around them. A major plus for individuals in this sign is that they are very good thinkers and are notable for coming up with brainstorming ideas that are geared at leaving others shocked to the bone marrows.
Their ideas are original and very straight to the point. A strong point for the individuals in this sign is that they appreciate intelligence and strong mental capabilities. The best way to get to them is through mental strength. They love to get involved with individuals

who possess strong mental abilities. They are not biased in passing judgment and as such, they will make very good critics. They do not get too emotional with things and people around them.

If Venus is at 06 degrees Capricorn

They are usually in charge of their emotions. They never let their emotions get the better part of them. The only time they tend to display their emotions is at the time when it is most needed. They do not really trust people around them especially people who tend to be too extravagant in the use of their actions.

These sets of individuals would rather make friends with individuals that are older than they are or people who occupy important positions in society. They respect people who occupy good positions and have a responsibility of duty to individuals who prefer to give in to passions and emotions. They pay more attention to respect and duty than any other emotional entanglement. Nonetheless, they need to be careful of emotions that are practical- based if not, they would end up as a lonely set of individuals.

If Mars is in 20 degrees Pisce

They find it difficult to assess themselves. They are very sensitive and are vulnerable to different situations. They sometimes get tired and require to rest at all times. But this doesn't mean that they are lazy. It is just a means for them to recover their strength and health. They are actually not lazy individuals and will actually do well if they let go of their ego.

Fortunately, these set of individuals do not turn a blind eye to the needs of others. They are not selfish and will do everything possible to help those around them. They also have the ability to give out to people without a grudge and without the intention of holding anything back in return.

There are times when they get the urge to play smart behind people back. This should be avoided at all costs as it can lead to their ultimate downfall.

If Jupiter is in 27 degrees Aries

They are very independent individuals and do not compromise their standards in any way. They always want an avenue to explore their skills and potentials. It is totally acceptable to give a try at every circumstance. They need to be able to discover their true self and acknowledge everything they have ever worked for. But they should never get carried away with their accomplishment that they forget the plight of others. More so, they need to build up the level of their self-discipline so that it can aid them to focus on their energies and how to get the best use of it.

If Saturn is in 10 degrees Taurus

They have a great sense of freedom and this sometimes causes discomfort to them. They also have a firm will and composure that carries them through all their activities. It is difficult for them to adapt to new situations and new events. They feel insecure most times and feel that there are certain things they do not have but really desire. These include emotional needs such as love, joy, happiness and so on.

The feeling of insecurity makes them feel insecure and act stingy towards others. When they surround themselves with people who are more supportive, they would become the best of their kind.

If Uranus is in 16 degrees Aquarius

They are willing to effect change in every aspect of life. Fortunately, the type of individuals they associate themselves with actually feel the same. They are desirous of making changes that would be for the cause of the greater good. They can go the extra mile to ensure it becomes a reality. With the right kind of support, they can actually achieve this. However, if they feel to monitor the desires to make the world a better place, they stand the risk of losing themselves to the pursuit of another form of interest. This would adversely affect their relationship with other individuals.

If Neptune is at 04 degrees Aquarius

They would be able to analyze any kind of given situation. Fortunately, they keep friends that share the same opinion as they do. They will always make effective decisions and take the right kind of steps to ensure that they help to right the wrongdoings in the society. Nonetheless, they need to strive to maintain the right kind of help and protect the interest of the concerned individuals.

If Pluto is in 12 degrees Sagarittus
The individuals in this sign are regarded as proponents of change. In their generation, there would be a lot of change that may do away with society's cherished beliefs.

There would be a lot of changes in conventional beliefs and way of life. The changes can also completely affect the traditional system, and this would bring about a huge change in society.

In their generation, a lot of individuals would also experience big changes that would affect their lives.

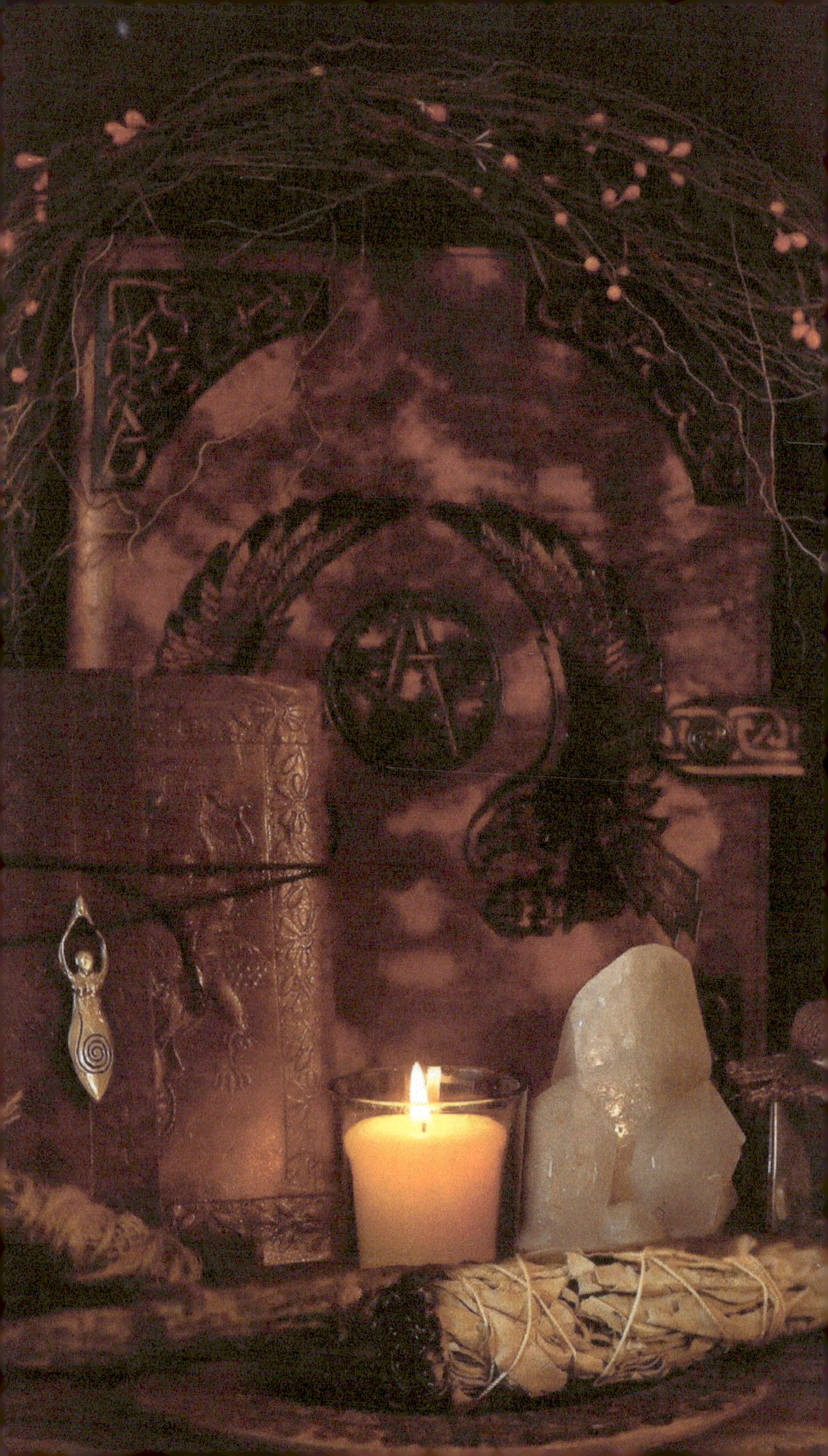

CHAPTER - 7
Wicca Altar and Tools and their symbology

When making your altar, after outfitting it with some of the traditional tools talked about in the other books of this series like:

- Athame
- Broom
- Candle
- Cauldron
- Chalice
- Incense
- Pentacle
- Wand

you may enjoy personalizing your new space by including some additional elements of your choosing. These additions will out rightly make your altar unique and personal.

You have to pick items that will significantly beautify

and align with your goal. Look out for things that resonate with your belief and desire in such a way that you will not worry about spending all the days at your altar. Here are some of the things you can include in your altar.

Minerals, Crystals, and Rocks

Like several others, you can decide to go with any of these, which many practitioners have been known to place on their altars. Crystals' exquisite natural forms, alongside their colors, highlight the transformational power of nature.

You can buy rocks and minerals c at specialty shops, but if you are on a budget, then you do not need to be worried. You can simply gather them on your own as a part of your practice. To do this, search for agates and jaspers on beaches and river beds. Then, proceed to look for signs of quartz, calcite, and other common minerals on public lands. The process is the most beautiful aspect of this.

Live Plants

Live plants have a way of adding health and vitality to any space. Thus, expecting their vibrancy at altars is not a mere wish. Get yourself a green thumb, place one or two small plants on your altar; they will breathe life and oxygen into your practice.

Use succulents and air plants if your altar is situated at a place it gets sufficient light, succulents These two types are preferred because of their small size and low maintenance requirements. To get a small plant, go to the nearest plant shops or ask people around you that are into horticulture.

Dried Herbs, Flowers, and Plants

Dried herbs and plants may be used in a variety of spells, rituals, and offerings, so keeping a selection on hand is always a good idea. Wander through natural areas and keep an eye out for useful herbs like rosemary and mint. These can be placed in your chalice or cauldron and left for a few days to dry. Hang gathered flowers upside down to dry, then place them on your altar for decoration and as a nod to the current season.

Animal Remains

When outside gathering materials for some of your other altar items, watch out for the remains of fallen animals. Look out for such things as bones, shed antlers, teeth, fur. These things can be found where these animals have chosen as an abode and have lost their lives.

However, if you are intent on getting them at all cost, then wooded areas in public lands away from main trails should be where you are headed. Animal remains can really the best altar adornment you need because of the energy of nature's diverse array of life and the way it reminds one of the certainties of death. Yet, you need to know your state and country laws before heading out because some countries find it illegal to scavenge the remains of some protected species.

Jewelry

You can also include Jewelry. There are various things you can add, like amulets, rings, brooches, and other adornments. To get the best connection to them, try to opt for the ones gifted to you by your family. This can easily make powerful additions to your magical arsenal. Also, when you place jewels, you cherish you are making it more personal, and adding a degree of elegance to its aesthetic.

Crafts and Drawings

Because creation is such an aspect of magic, you can include things you drew, painted, sculpted, assembled, or otherwise. You can also make periodical changes of your altar if you are an artist or one that creates things frequently. If you like, you can simply display older pieces for the reconnection of forgotten times or feelings.

In case you have not created any real thing, you can use this opportunity to make one of the classic altar tools like the wand, broom, or pentacle.

Any Other Thing You Want To Include

When it comes to the assemblage and decoration of your altar, there are no rules, so feel absolutely free to include anything and everything not mentioned in this

list, so long as it contributes to your altar in one of the following ways:
- It gives you a reason to enjoy spending time at your altar.
- It personalizes your altar.
- It helps in the direction of your energy or intention.
- It has a significant function in your life or practice.
- It enables you to focus on your goals.

Here is a list of things you might want to include.

Representations of deities

You can place things like pictures, candles, a statue, etc. Now, if you are one that honors a single god, you can put things that represent them there. But if you enjoy worshiping multiple deities, merely lining up their various symbols at the back of the altar will do just fine.

Representations of the Elements

These things can be a small cluster between the symbols of the deities you are worshiping. Make the edges of the altar be the chosen area.

For Air

A censer, fan, feather, etc. They are masculine elements and can be placed on the right.

For Earth
A bowl of salt, cornmeal, sand, etc. They are feminine elements and can be placed on the left, representing the goddesses.

For Fire
A candle, lava rock, electric candle, etc. Same as the air. It can be placed on the right edge of the altar.

For Water
A bowl of water, seashell, small mirror, etc. Just like the earth, it can be placed on the left side of the altar

Miscellaneous Items

You can place them anywhere that feels appropriate. Logically, you might want to put taller items like the candle materials at the back of the altar while the smaller ones are allowed to fill in different spaces. And for larger round things like your large basins or cauldron can stay at the center.

Remember: these are simply suggestions, you have the right to do things as you deem fit. Some examples of miscellaneous objects are:
- Candle Materials: Service candle (a white taper to light all other stuff); candleholders.
- Food Items: Libation dish; cakes and ale, etc.
- Spiritual objects: Crystals, charms, talismans,

etc.; divination tools; spell components;
- Decorations: Flowers, holiday decorations, etc.

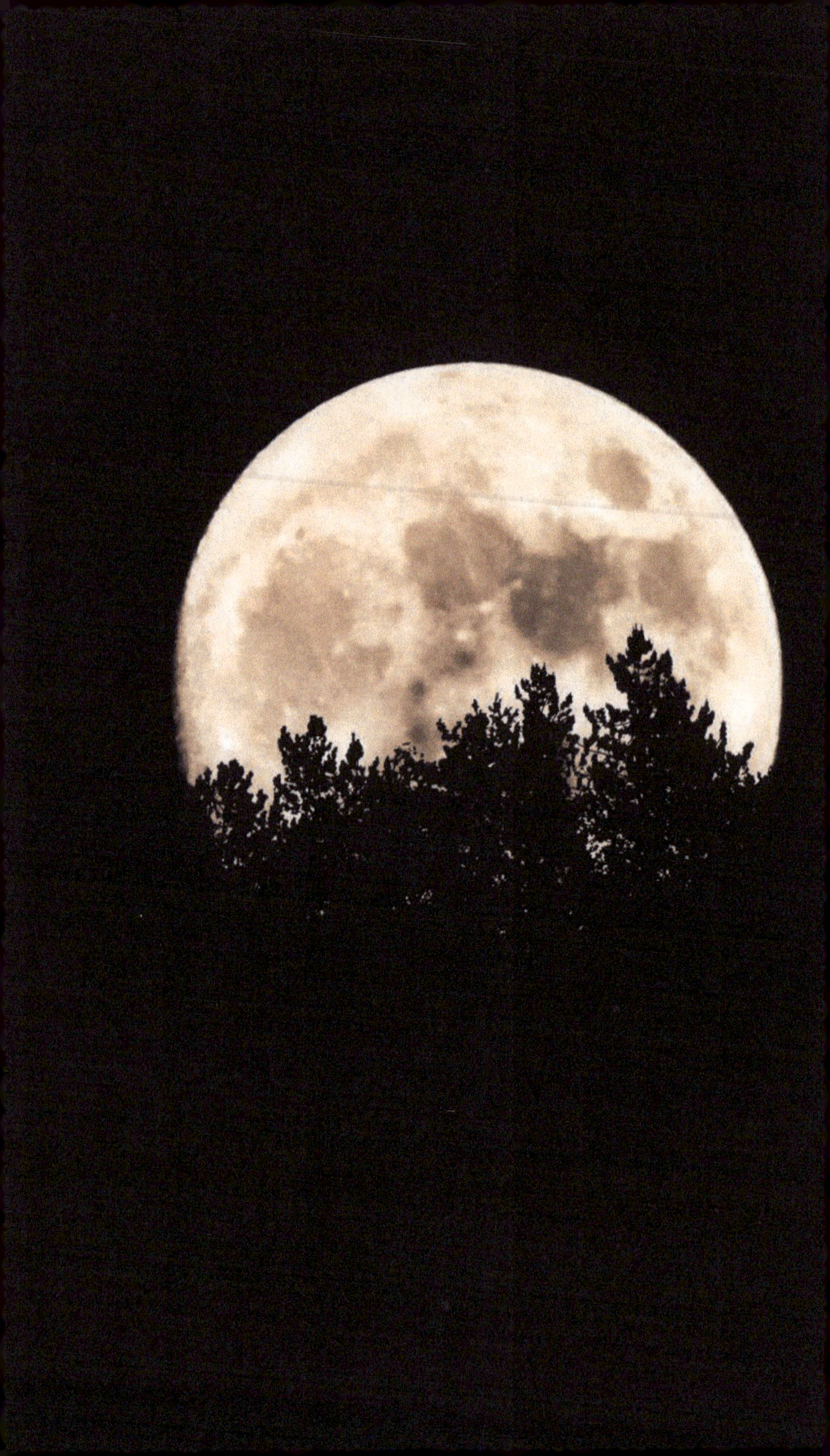

CONCLUSION

Wiccan is a religious practice that accommodates a lot of spiritual activity. In this religion, there are a lot of factors and elements that you need to take cognizance of. It is a spiritual- centered activity that is graced with a lot of divine beings.

A Wiccan altar is a sacred place where spells and rituals are performed. The religion is strongly hinged on positivity and the desire to bring forth the very best of an individual. Unlike what most people think, Wiccan is not an act of paganism. It is a religious practice that encourages the use of nature to maintain a close relationship with the divine beings.

Endeavor to keep the altar clean and ensure that you also purify yourself before commencing with any spell. It is always important that you understand the various types of spell and how you can make use of it.

Casting a Wiccan spell requires that you take cognizance of certain factors such as the items involved for the ritual and the steps to casting a spell. There are different spells for different purposes. Some of the spells have their consequences and it is important that you know exactly what you are getting yourself into.

Wiccan is a religious practice that makes use of astrology. Wiccans are encouraged to make use of their astrological signs to get the desired results from any spell or ritual they cast. Birth months are usually used as a means of identifying the best way to cast a Wiccan spell.

An understanding of the astrological signs helps to make it possible for the Wiccan practitioner to cast the spell with the right methods.

This was

WICCA SYMBOLS FOR BEGINNERS

the Third book in Wicca Altar and Tools Series. Please be sure to check out the other 2 books from the same series.

WICCA ALTAR FOR BEGINNERS

WICCA TOOLS FOR BEGINNERS

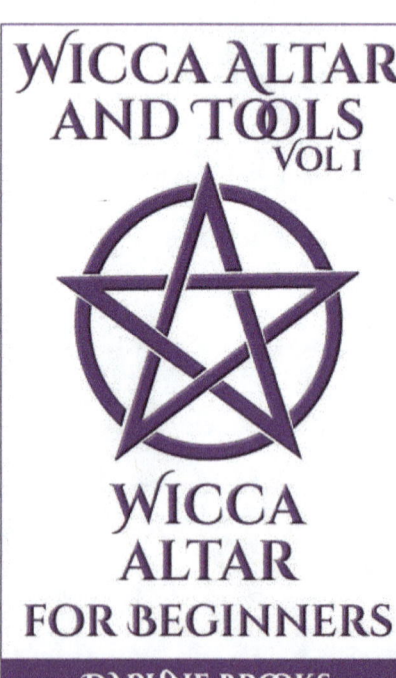

Please consider leaving a great
5-Star review for this book

CPSIA information can be obtained
at www.ICGtesting.com
Printed in the USA
BVHW011046120221
599999BV00001B/6